Unsolved
Celebrity
Mysteries

Mysteries and Conspiracies™

UNSOLVED CELEBRITY MYSTERIES

David Southwell and Sean Twist

ROSEN
PUBLISHING®

New York

North American edition first published in 2008 by:

The Rosen Publishing Group, Inc.
29 East 21st Street
New York, NY 10010

North American edition book design: Tom Forget

Library of Congress Cataloging-in-Publication Data

Southwell, David, 1971–
[Conspiracy theories]
Unsolved celebrity mysteries / David Southwell and Sean Twist.—North American ed.
      p.cm.—(Mysteries and Conspiracies)
Includes index.
ISBN-13: 978-1-4042-1082-0
ISBN-10: 1-4042-1082-2
1. Conspiracies. 2. Celebrities—Miscellanea.
I. Twist, Sean. II. Title.
HV6275.S56 2008
001.9—dc22

                                                        2007007685

Manufactured in the United States of America

On the cover: Kurt Cobain *(left)* and Bruce Lee *(right)* are two celebrities whose deaths have been surrounded by conspiracy theories.

CONTENTS

1 KURT COBAIN

At 8:40 am on April 8, 1994, an electrician who had come to fit security lighting to a luxury home in Seattle found the body of Kurt Cobain. A shotgun wound to the head had killed him. Beside his body was found a box of drug paraphernalia, including syringes and burnt spoons. A shotgun lay across his chest, and it was claimed a "good-bye" note was found in the room. An open-and-shut case of suicide then? Only for the local police. Conspiriologists were hardly going to be satisfied with the cursory examination of Seattle's boys in blue and the media frenzy of reporting following Cobain's untimely end.

The twenty-seven-year-old lead singer and songwriter of Nirvana was not only an internationally acclaimed rock star but an icon and inspiration to many members of Generation X. His fans viewed him as more than another star; to them he was a leader, a hero. His funeral brought Seattle to a state of

Kurt Cobain — was his death suicide or murder?

gridlock, and there were copycat suicides across the world. Cobain died at the peak of his power. His music had reached out and touched millions, and incredible success had brought him the unwanted status of spokesman for a generation as well as the grunge rock movement.

Punk rock was an escape for Cobain; drugs were an escape for Cobain. At first it seemed entirely in keeping with his character that he might have sought death as the ultimate escape from the pain and depression that had dogged him throughout his young life. However, despite the common knowledge that Cobain was a troubled man, many have found it hard to believe that he took his own life and conspiracy theories concerning his demise have proliferated while his records continue to sell.

The common thread in the numerous allegations in circulation is that despite his troubled state of mind—exemplified by a close shave with death via a heroin overdose in a Rome hotel a month before—Cobain actually was starting to sort himself out and plan positive changes in his life. A messy divorce from his wife and fellow rock star Courtney Love and a high-profile custody battle for their daughter may have been in the cards, but Cobain was not one to wimp out. He had shown toughness before and was a man who had fought his way from a backwoods redneck town to global status. Many of those who have studied the case feel that sinister forces were working in Seattle to ensure an untimely end for Cobain. They have certainly come up with some unsettling questions surrounding his alleged suicide.

Courtney Love, Kurt's widow, hired a private detective to find her missing husband.

THE STRANGE PART

On Easter Sunday, April 3, 1994, Courtney Love called Tom Grant, a California-based private detective. The previous day Cobain had climbed over the wall of Exodus rehab clinic and had flown back to Seattle. Despite the fact that her husband was known to be suicidal, had almost died in an overdose less than a month before, and was returning to a home containing a shotgun, Love decided not to go to Seattle to find him herself. Instead, she hired Grant and dispatched him to track down Cobain with the rather flippant and enigmatic phrase, "Save the American icon, Tom." Grant searched for Cobain at the Seattle house on April 7, at 2:45 AM and 9:45 PM, but did not find the body that was hidden in the greenhouse on top of the garage. It was eventually discovered the next day.

THE USUAL SUSPECTS

Someone Close to Kurt

Tom Grant, whom Love subsequently hired for seven months to investigate Cobain's death, is just one of many who believe that Cobain must have been murdered by someone close to him. Given that the murderer and other conspirators must have had his trust and good access to him, many theorists believe the finger points to a family member, close friend, or employee.

Record Industry Executives

It is widely rumored that Cobain was more concerned about leaving the music industry than leaving the world of the living. A dead rock icon is worth a lot more in terms of back catalogue sales than a live one who is no longer interested in a music career. Record industry executives are well-known for possessing a moral sense that makes alley cats look like upstanding members of the community, and with millions of dollars at stake, murder might have been seen as preferable to Cobain's retirement.

THE UNUSUAL SUSPECTS

Kurt Cobain

It would not be a rock 'n' roll conspiracy theory if there were not some conspiriologists who believe that Cobain is still alive. The inconsistencies surrounding his apparent death can be fully explained by his faking it to escape from his wife, by the pressures of being a celebrity, and by the drugs scene.

Military-Industrial Complex

Cobain's role as spokesman for a generation that was apathetic about political concerns could have made him a danger to the military-industrial complex (MIC) if he had decided to galvanize the disaffected young of the globe by taking an antiwar stance over the developing conflict in Yugoslavia. To ensure healthy weapon sales and lack of public interest, a preemptive strike may have been called for.

MOST CONVINCING EVIDENCE

There is a whole raft of hard crime-scene evidence that raises questions over the idea that Cobain killed himself. One of his credit cards was missing and someone had attempted to use it after the time the autopsy says he was shot and before the body was discovered. There were no fingerprints on the shotgun or shells, which suggests the weapon had been wiped, and his body was found to contain an incapacitating level of heroin that should have prevented him from being able to fire the gun. The "suicide" note was actually a note explaining why he was quitting the record industry, and many handwriting experts believe that someone other than Cobain added the last four lines relating to his wife and daughter.

MOST MYSTERIOUS FACT

It has been reported that a "Dream Machine"—a trance-inducing contraption made from a lightbulb, record player, and cardboard cylinder with slits in it—was found in the greenhouse with Cobain. Brion Gysin, a friend and collaborator with author William S. Burroughs—one of Cobain's acknowledged heroes—first created the Dream Machine. A group calling themselves Friends Understanding Kurt have pointed out that there have been previously recorded incidents where the use of a Dream Machine has been associated with suicides.

SKEPTICALLY SPEAKING

A deeply troubled man with an enormous drug habit and an interest in firearms—that makes it just so hard to understand why anyone thinks Cobain may have taken his own life, doesn't it? Given that he was once photographed with a gun in his mouth, Cobain actually pulling the trigger one day isn't exactly the most surprising ending to his story. It might be a puzzle for some to figure out why people buy Britney Spears's records, but even with the odd circumstances surrounding Cobain's end, there is little mystery about why the sharp money is on suicide in this case.

2 THE ASSASSINATION OF JFK

November 22, 1963, is a day not easily forgotten. Even now, countless millions of people can recall what they were doing on the day President John F. Kennedy was shot.

It was a bright, clear, and almost summerlike day in Dallas. The sky above the Texas School Book Depository was free from clouds. There could be no better day for a parade to welcome the president, and yet, within seconds, several bullets had struck the presidential limousine at Dealey Plaza, and history was changed forever.

Despite the suppression of vast amounts of evidence and the best attempts of the Warren Commission in the aftermath of the assassination to promote the idea that JFK was killed by Lee Harvey Oswald acting alone, 73 percent of Americans believe that their president was the victim of a conspiracy.

President Kennedy on that fateful day in Dallas — just moments before his death.

It's a view that is backed up by the report of the Select Committee on Assassinations of the House of Representatives, which states: "The Committee believes, on the basis of the evidence available to it, that President John F. Kennedy was assassinated as the result of a conspiracy."

A close look at the assassination of JFK produces convincing evidence that Oswald was not acting alone and that a cover-up at the highest levels is still in operation. It becomes more a question of who was behind the conspiracy than whether it was a conspiracy at all.

THE STRANGE PART

Despite the official government opinion that the president was killed by a single shot, there were seven wounds found on JFK and on Governor Connally, one of the other passengers in the car. The angles and trajectories of the wounds make a single gunman fairly unfeasible. Lee Harvey Oswald, who was arrested for the murder, was himself assassinated before he could be brought to trial.

THE USUAL SUSPECTS

The CIA

Kennedy was about to disband the CIA due to its corruption, its inability to oust Castro from Cuba, and its general hostility to him since the Bay of Pigs debacle. It is alleged that, in self-defense, the CIA plotted with the Mafia and FBI to kill Kennedy and frame a former double agent, Oswald, as the killer.

Cuban Communists/KGB

Fidel Castro and his KGB allies were still smarting from Kennedy's victory in the Cuban Missile Crisis. As revenge, they plotted his murder. Their involvement in his death was discovered by the CIA and FBI, who had to cover it up to prevent a public outrage that could have led to World War III.

Mafia

JFK and his attorney general brother, Robert Kennedy, were close to winning their crusade against organized crime. Attempts to blackmail Kennedy over his adultery had failed, so the Mafia decided to have him rubbed out. It is known that Oswald had connections to Mafia members; just why did small-time Dallas mobster Jack Ruby so conveniently shoot Oswald?

Military-Industrial Complex

Kennedy had plans to pull out of Vietnam. This obviously angered the military-industrial complex, which thrives on war. Were connections in the shadowy worlds of the Secret Service and Mafia used to conduct a coup and place Vice President Johnson in the White House? Interestingly, just four days after JFK's assassination, Johnson sent more troops to Vietnam, completely ignoring JFK's recommendations.

Also suspected: the Masons; MJ-12 (Majestic 12, the top-secret defense committee overseeing America's negotiations with the aliens that do all those abductions); Richard Nixon; and the American oil barons.

THE UNUSUAL SUSPECTS

The Canadian Liberal Party

Over the years, evidence has emerged linking prominent Mafia captain Lucien Rivard to both Jack Ruby and the

Liberal Party of Canada. Rivard is also linked to Oswald's recorded time in Montreal. When the Mafia man was jailed in 1964 to await extradition to the United States, officers of the Canadian Justice Department, and members of the ruling Liberal Party, offered bribes to the American lawyers to try and secure his release. Despite the lack of motive, this has been enough for some people to suggest that the true answer to the conspiracy to assassinate JFK will be found in Canada.

Jackie Kennedy

The wildest and most discredited conspiracy theory surrounding the assassination is that Jackie Kennedy, sickened by her husband's continuous adultery, arranged for the Mafia to wipe him out and spare her the public humiliation of a divorce.

MOST CONVINCING EVIDENCE

One thing that swings it in the favor of the conspiracy theories is the impossibility of the "single bullet theory" accepted by the Warren Commission. It claimed that the one shot Oswald took from a sixth-floor window entered Kennedy's back, yet rose and flew out of his neck, altering its trajectory to cause the seven wounds found in Kennedy and Governor Connally, in the seat ahead of the president's.

MOST MYSTERIOUS FACT

President Kennedy's brain went missing under mysterious circumstances a number of years ago. This is highly suspicious and also very convenient, as modern scientific tests cannot now be carried out to establish the trajectory of the fatal bullets. The tests would have answered once and for all the question of whether there was a second (or even a third) gunman.

SKEPTICALLY SPEAKING

The legendary grassy knoll from where the second gunman was supposed to have shot Kennedy would have been so busy that surely someone would have spotted the thirty or so gunmen that would have been there to account for all the proposed conspiracy theories.

3 BRUCE LEE

Sometimes death does not end the web of intrigue that has grown up around a celebrity during his life. In fact, sometimes death is only the start of greater and stranger speculations.

In late July 1973, when they laid to rest the body of Bruce Lee, dressed in the Chinese costume he wore in the movie *Enter the Dragon*, in Seattle's Lakeview Cemetery, they did not succeed in burying the mystery surrounding his death.

A much-loved but controversial figure who made many enemies, Lee was thirty-two and at the height of his career when he suddenly died after falling into a coma. The subsequent coroner's report was inconclusive, and the numerous medical experts who looked at the case could only agree on one thing—that death had been brought about by a swelling of his brain.

On the fateful day of his death, Lee met film producer Raymond Chow at his home in the early afternoon and spent a couple of hours working with him on the film *The Game of Death*. The pair then went over to the home of Taiwanese actress Betty Tingpei, who was starring in the movie. Chow left for a meeting and Lee complained of having a headache. Tingpei gave him an Equagesic tablet—a form of powerful aspirin—and he took a nap. Chow rang Tingpei to invite her and Lee out for dinner, but the actress could not wake the sleeping star. By the time Lee arrived at the Queen Elizabeth Hospital, he was dead.

Dr. Lycette of the hospital felt that the death was a result of Lee being hypersensitive to compounds in the Equagesic tablet, but other medical authorities disagreed and rumors of a conspiracy began to spread throughout Hong Kong and the rest of the martial arts world.

THE STRANGE PART

Months before he was officially declared dead, rumors had been circulating around Hong Kong that Lee had died. These grew so strong that journalists at one of Hong Kong's largest newspapers wouldn't believe he was alive until they had spoken personally to Lee and subjected him to some rigorous questioning. This does tend to suggest that his eventual death may not have been as unexpected as the official version of events suggests.

THE USUAL SUSPECTS

The Triads

In the seventies, Chinese criminal organizations, such as the Triads, often demanded protection money from Hong Kong–based movie stars. Lee was known to have stood up to their demands and may have been poisoned as a result of this brave move—he was so adored by the Hong Kong public that he had to be disposed of in a subtle way.

Secret Martial Arts Masters

A popular and plausible conjecture is that Lee was killed on the instructions of a cabal of secret martial arts masters who were angered that he had taught too many of their secrets to foreigners. It is true that Lee already had many problems with the traditional Chinese martial arts establishment. Given the nature of the dim mak known to these masters, this theory is not easily dismissed. (Dim mak is a death touch that can be administered by glancing contact and is impossible for an autopsy to detect.) Also suspected: a secret group of Hong Kong movie producers; a cabal of Hollywood Masons; Chinese Communists; defeated opponents; and the British Intelligence Service.

Thirty years after his death, Bruce Lee remains a martial arts legend.

THE UNUSUAL SUSPECTS

Ancient Chinese Demons

It is rumored that Lee felt his family was suffering from an ancient curse that ensured that the firstborn son of any generation would be haunted by demons. The tradition of this curse in his family was so strong that when Bruce was born, he was originally given a girl's name to confuse the demonic powers. More than one conspiracy theorist feels that this theory has been strengthened by the strange case of the death of Brandon Lee, Bruce's son, who died after a mysterious handgun accident during the filming of the movie blockbuster *The Crow*.

Bruce Lee

An even wilder conspiracy theory proposes that Lee is still alive and that he staged his supposed death in an attempt to escape from either the pressures of fame or the evil intent of various Triad gangs. Those that believe this hypothesis also think that Lee may return at some unspecified point in the future. He certainly is not spotted as much as Elvis.

Lee's son, Brandon, died under mysterious circumstances during the shooting of the movie *The Crow*.

MOST CONVINCING EVIDENCE

One thing that persuades many that there is a conspiracy behind Bruce Lee's death is the confusion over the medical evidence surrounding his demise. The coroner's report proved inconclusive, and the medical authorities put forward no less than five different theories to explain what caused the swelling of the brain that led to his untimely death.

MOST MYSTERIOUS FACT

When interviewed, Lee frequently reflected on the possibility of an early death and at times almost appeared to welcome it. His wife, Linda, is quoted as saying that Bruce had no wish to live to old age as he found the prospect of losing his physical abilities too horrifying to contemplate. Death as an escape from failing strength and fading prowess as a master of martial arts combat may not have been the only reason Lee contemplated dying young. It is known that he took the idea of the firstborn of his family being cursed by demons seriously enough to try and protect his son Brandon by employing traditional magic.

SKEPTICALLY SPEAKING

Much of the speculation of the circumstances surrounding the conspiracy can be explained by the fact that when Raymond

Chow announced Lee's death on television, he omitted the fact that he had not died at home but in the apartment of Betty Tingpei. The attempt to cover up this possibly embarrassing detail may have led many people to become convinced that there was a lot more going on behind the scenes, especially when there was an unsolved medical puzzle over the exact cause of the fatal swelling of the brain.

4 THE SHOOTING OF JOHN LENNON

In the "do you remember where you were when you heard the news?" stakes, the shooting of John Lennon comes second only to the assassination of JFK or the events of 9/11. If you were alive when the murder of John Lennon was announced on the evening of December 8, 1980, you will undoubtedly remember it, wherever you were. As the news broke around the globe, everyone was shocked. No one could understand why anyone would want to kill one of the members of the most beloved musical groups of all time. Why would anyone want to murder an ex-Beatle? Why would anyone want to deny the world this true musical genius and very influential campaigner for peace?

The explanation offered in the press was that the gunman—Mark David Chapman—was a disturbed loner, obsessed with the sixties star and convinced that Lennon was in league with the devil. After a sixty-day psychiatric

John Lennon and Yoko Ono. His radical politics could have made him a target.

evaluation that turned into a year and sixty days of absolute silence, Chapman pleaded guilty to the murder a matter of hours before his trial was scheduled to start.

It wasn't long before conspiracy theorists were supplementing the media's version of events with their own interpretations of what actually happened on the tragic night that robbed the world of a cultural giant. In their eyes, the shooting was not simply the work of a madman; it was part of a huge political plot.

THE STRANGE PART

One of the usual reasons put forward for why people like Chapman murder celebrities is that they wish to become famous themselves. This obviously is not the case with Chapman. Since he committed the crime, he has turned down more than sixty interviews and repeatedly said, "I do not want publicity." He has given only one major interview and that was merely to ask to be released after he failed to get parole in October 2003. His apparent calmness after his arrest was unusual. However, more significant is the fact that he managed to evade metal detectors at two major airports when transporting the murder weapon from Hawaii to New York—something bound to raise alarm bells with those favoring a conspiracy as an explanation for Lennon's death.

THE USUAL SUSPECTS

The FBI

The late FBI director J. Edgar Hoover had a pathological hatred of Lennon and had tried to persuade President Nixon's chief of staff to help him bust the musician and get him thrown out of the country. The FBI kept Lennon under close scrutiny throughout the seventies and tried to thwart his attempts to gain U.S. citizenship. Many of their files on him are still classified, some because they are linked to British Intelligence information on Lennon. If there was a conspiracy to kill the singer, it is not unreasonable to deduce that the FBI may have played a part in it.

Right-Wing Activists/Military-Industrial Complex

Reagan just had been elected president, and some felt that opposition to his aggressive foreign policy and plans to spend massive amounts of the budget on expanding the American military was bound to develop around veteran peace campaigner Lennon. In fear of Lennon inspiring the youth to rebel, as he had done in the sixties, right-wing activists and certain sections of the military-industrial complex plotted to silence him.

The CIA

Chapman had worked for defense companies with close links to the CIA. He also showed some evidence of having been hypnotized. In this light, some have looked in the direction of the CIA's outlawed project to create programmed killers—MK-Ultra—for the real reason Chapman murdered his former hero.

THE UNUSUAL SUSPECTS

Satanic Forces

Lennon was shot outside the Dakota building—an apartment block that had provided the backdrop to Roman Polanski's film about the birth of the Antichrist, *Rosemary's Baby*.

Beatles music and lyrics were used as elements in Charles Manson's warped reasoning that eventually led to the ritual killing of Roman Polanski's wife, Sharon Tate. David Mark Chapman believed that Lennon was, in fact, the Antichrist. These spooky synchronicities have been enough to produce wild claims that the shooting was the result of machinations carried out by satanic forces or members of a satanic cult that caused Chapman to be possessed.

Christian Fundamentalists

Mark David Chapman was not the only one who thought Lennon was the Antichrist. Ever since Lennon's "more popular than Jesus" quote, certain American fundamentalists believed the ex-Beatle was a dark force dedicated to corrupting the youth of America by spreading a gospel of love, drugs, and rock 'n' roll. With Lennon's return to the spotlight after a self-imposed period as a househusband, it may be that they decided to silence him once and for all.

MOST CONVINCING EVIDENCE

The strength of the fight put up by the FBI against those using the Freedom of Information Act (FOIA) to try to force the agency to make public its files on the singer is suspicious. So, too, is the fact that even now not all of the material on the files has been disclosed. Given that the FBI claims the reason its files cannot be made public is to protect national security, previously paranoid-sounding claims made by conspiracy buffs may have more veracity than it is comfortable to believe.

MOST MYSTERIOUS FACT

Conspiracy theorists who believe that Paul McCartney is dead and has been replaced with a look-alike examine the Beatles' lyrics and album covers in search of clues. In a similar way, fringe researchers into the mystery surrounding Lennon's death also have found significance in certain publicity photos and songs. In the booklet that came with the original *Magical Mystery Tour* album in the United States, there is a picture of John and a sign next to him stating: "The best way to go is by MD&C." Given these are the initials of Mark David Chapman, some have seen this as either a strange example of synchronicity or a massive clue signposting an astonishing conspiracy.

SKEPTICALLY SPEAKING

The proposed conspiracy theories all go out of their way to overlook the obvious fact that America's lax attitude to gun control laws and a mentally disturbed man who had an obsession with Lennon are enough of a dangerous combination to provide all the explanation you could ever possibly need.

5 PAUL MCCARTNEY

When you are one of the most famous musicians in the world and your name is known to anyone who has ever listened to pop music, you cannot be too surprised when strange rumors spring up around you—it is the nature of modern celebrity.

In the latter half of the sixties, a rumor spread through the media, and consequently the rest of the Beatle-loving world, that Paul McCartney was actually dead and that an impostor, named William Campbell, was put in his place.

The alleged conspiracy was first exposed to the public by Detroit disc jockey Russ Gibb. He advised his listeners to seek for clues in the band's music, even if it entailed playing the record backwards. One such "clue" is allegedly featured in the "Number nine, number nine" lyric from "Revolution 9" on the Beatles' *White Album*, which apparently becomes "Turn me on dead man" when played backwards.

The rumor grew faster than Yoko Ono's hair. Millions of Beatles fans, and those who wanted a new hobby, spent hours of their time looking for new clues that revealed that Paul was dead. People were looking for evidence of a conspiracy in everything remotely related to the Beatles. Every clue confirmed what many suspected—Paul McCartney was dead and there was a huge conspiracy to conceal this fact.

THE STRANGE PART

On the classic *Sergeant Pepper's Lonely Hearts' Club Band* album, Paul is wearing an arm patch with the initials OPD—commonly recognized as an acronym for Officially Pronounced Dead.

THE USUAL SUSPECTS

The Beatles

Conspiracy theorists of a more skeptical bent have concluded that there are in fact many clues to Paul's death scattered throughout the musical output of the Beatles, but that they have been placed there by the Beatles as a metaphysical hoax. They believe that Paul died spiritually and was reborn in the ways of the maharishi. This spiritual rebirth and his old self dying became an in-joke among the group, and they placed obscure references to it on their album covers and in the lyrics of their songs.

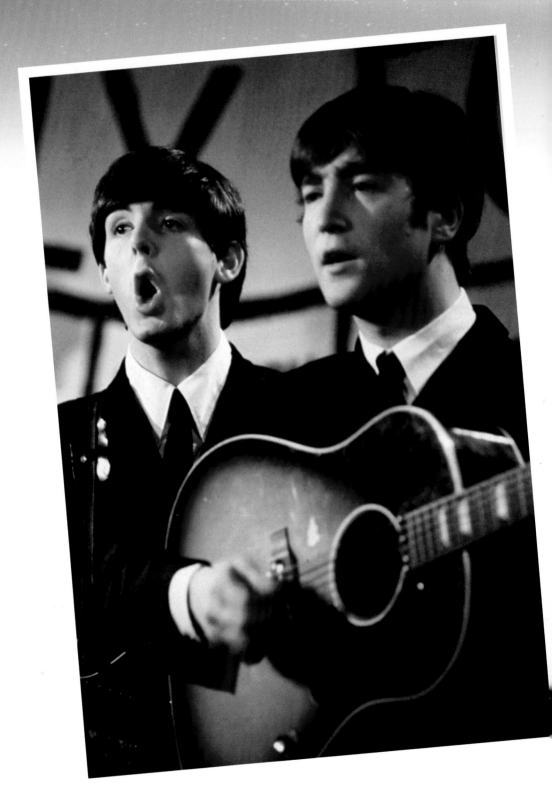

The Record Company

Mass hysteria was created by the rumor that Paul was dead. People fanatically searched for clues and evidence and went to ridiculous lengths to find them. More than one conspiracy theorist has suggested that it was all a hoax cooked up by the record company to help sustain interest in the Beatles. If this is correct, it certainly qualifies as one of the most fascinating publicity stunts of all time. Even those who feel the conspiracy theory is a hoax still love hearing the clues.

The CIA

Many people claim that the CIA wanted to bring an end to the Beatles' powerful influence on the world. They may have seen the Beatles and their massive, almost religious, following as a threat to society, which had already witnessed the outrage that John Lennon's comments on the Beatles being "more popular than Jesus" had created. The Beatles were undoubtedly musical and social gods in the sixties and may have been seen as a threat to the established order by the agency. The agency's attempt to destroy the Beatles by murdering Paul was not completely successful as the other three Beatles enrolled the services of William Campbell, the winner of a Paul McCartney look-alike contest.

The real Paul McCartney *(left)* or an impostor named William Campbell?

THE UNUSUAL SUSPECTS

Elvis Presley

A less grounded theory is that Elvis Presley employed the CIA to murder Paul. It has been claimed that Presley had been jealous and threatened by the Beatles' success from the day that the Beatles first set foot in the United States. He was the "King of Rock 'n' Roll" and no one was going to take that title away from him. So, maybe he went to the extreme measure of sanctioning Paul McCartney's assassination. Elvis was popular among the highest politicians in the American government and had extremely powerful contacts. Therefore, if he had been behind McCartney's alleged death, it would be unlikely that he would face any "Jailhouse Rock" for his crime.

The Devil

Another possible explanation was first proposed by the American academic professor Glazier, who suggested that the devil killed Paul as repayment for a bargain he had struck with McCartney for the Beatles' immense success in the world. Obviously, rock stars were not the only horned beasts running around during the sixties. Paul is said to have suffered the same fate as Brian Jones of the Rolling Stones, who also paid the price of success.

MOST CONVINCING EVIDENCE

The cover of the *Abbey Road* album was declared as evidence of Paul's death by Fred LaBour in *The Michigan Daily*.

He claimed that the Beatles were depicted as a type of funeral group who were leaving the cemetery. John, dressed in white, represented a minister. George was a grave-digger, and Ringo was an undertaker. Paul, of course, was the corpse, who was barefoot and out of step with the others, suggesting an impostor was present.

MOST MYSTERIOUS FACT

Among the many lyrics that could have been related to Paul's death, one in particular stands out. In the song "Glass Onion," John Lennon sings the words "The Walrus was Paul." It has been claimed that "walrus" means "corpse" in Greek.

SKEPTICALLY SPEAKING

The quality of the so-called clues is exceptionally dubious. *The Abbey Road* album cover features the license plate 28 IF—which some have interpreted as being Paul's age if he had lived—but if Paul was still alive, he would have been twenty-seven, not twenty-eight. Many of the records that were played backwards sounded so strange and vague that almost any phrase could have fitted with the sound. It is all a case of looking so hard for something that you are guaranteed to find it. No impostor would have been able to duplicate McCartney's exceptional musical talent, though some conspiracy theorists argue that Paul's solo career is the ultimate proof of their claims.

6 Marilyn Monroe— Death of a Goddess

On May 19, 1962, President John F. Kennedy enjoyed a very public birthday celebration at New York's famous Madison Square Garden. At the celebrity-studded bash, more than 15,000 people saw Marilyn Monroe sing "Happy Birthday" to JFK in breathless, sexual whispers that have entered into pop-culture legend.

Just a few months later, on August 4, 1962, the thirty-six-year-old woman, born as Norma Jean Mortenson, was dead—found naked amid her silk sheets, an empty bottle of powerful barbiturates on her dressing table. Marilyn Monroe was a true Hollywood legend and probably the world's first global sex symbol, yet behind the legend is a tragic story of a tortured soul—an alcoholic who had been abused by all of the famous, powerful men in her life. Everything pointed toward the fact that the star had taken her own life.

On the other hand, some have always felt that Marilyn's suicide was just a little too neat and convenient, especially for a range of interested parties such as JFK, Robert F. Kennedy, the Mafia, the CIA, and the FBI—who all had good reasons for wanting her to be kept permanently silent. The best way for a murder to go undiscovered is for it to look like an accident or a suicide. Conspiracy theorists have never believed Marilyn Monroe deliberately or accidentally took her own life. Remarkably, one thing that almost all those who believe Monroe was murdered agree on is that if she was killed, it was probably done while she was held down with pillows and injected in the foot with barbiturates.

THE STRANGE PART

It became well known in the years following her death that Marilyn had a very close relationship with both John and Bobby Kennedy and that the CIA and FBI were keeping her under surveillance, both as a possible threat to national security and as a risk to the president's reputation. Given the level of their involvement in monitoring the star and the clear suggestion that evidence about her last few days of life had been tampered with or covered up, a plot to murder Marilyn is not entirely without credibility.

THE USUAL SUSPECTS

The CIA

The CIA was keeping Marilyn under surveillance because her intimate relationship with JFK meant that she had knowledge that made her a potential threat to national security. Whether this concerned the CIA's use of the Mafia to try and eliminate Castro and blackmail other heads of state is unknown, but the CIA's interest in the blonde bombshell is as certain as is its agents' ability to carry out a discrete murder.

The Mafia

Having an intimate relationship with JFK, Attorney General Robert F. Kennedy, and various high-powered members of the Mafia—including the mighty Sam Giancana—Marilyn knew things that could have destroyed the most powerful people in the United States. When her usefulness to the Mafia had run its course with the end of her relationship with Robert F. Kennedy, the Mafia may have felt she was a dangerous loose cannon that needed silencing.

The FBI

Marilyn had been attempting to blackmail RFK into continuing their affair and may have been attempting a more audacious blackmail of JFK—threatening to expose the fact that he had only become president with the vote-fixing aid of the Chicago mob. FBI boss J. Edgar Hoover was no friend of the Kennedy family, but as a self-styled patriot may have been happy to solve their problem with Monroe, to save

Marilyn Monroe sings to President Kennedy at Madison Square Garden in 1962.

the nation from scandal. Once he had arranged for Marilyn's death, he could control the upstart Kennedy brothers, forcing them to allow him to remain as head of the bureau that had effectively become his own private police force.

THE UNUSUAL SUSPECTS

The Catholic Church

One organization that the Kennedy clan trusted completely and that had links to the CIA and the mob was the Catholic Church. JFK was the United States' first Catholic president and the Church was keen to ensure that nothing threatened its man in the White House. Some have suggested that the desire to protect him even went as far as arranging for the death of his troublesome former girlfriend.

Men in Black

If the prospect of the original men in black—Catholic priests—is not unusual enough, there are some who have suggested that Marilyn was eliminated by the actual Men in Black, who are charged with keeping the lid on the UFO conspiracy. If JFK knew the truth about extraterrestrial life, he might have told Marilyn and thereby set in motion the chain of events that led up to her death when she became uncontrollable and liable to reveal the secrets he had shared with her.

MOST CONVINCING EVIDENCE

In recent years, legal documents dating from 1960 have come to light. These documents seem to prove that the Kennedy family promised to give Marilyn Monroe $600,000 in a trust fund for her mother, Gladys Baker, if Marilyn kept quiet about what she knew of the links between JFK and Mafia boss Sam Giancana. After the star died, it appears as if this pledge was broken and all references to it were covered up. These documents quickly became the subject of a hotly fought court action in the United States. Debate about their authenticity still rages. However, tests on the paper, ink, and signatures have all suggested that the documents are valid. If this is the case, they are the strongest evidence to come to light that the Kennedy clan may have had a hand in the star's death.

MOST MYSTERIOUS FACT

There are a lot of rumors, and more than a dash of good circumstantial evidence, to suggest that among the last visitors Marilyn received at her home were Bobby Kennedy and Hollywood actor Peter Lawford—who was married to Pat Kennedy Lawford and was therefore part of the Kennedy clan. By all accounts, Lawford and Kennedy were accompanied by an enigmatic third man who was dressed in black and carried a medical-style bag. The identity of this mysterious figure

Peter Lawford *(center)* and Robert Kennedy *(right)* were among the last people to see Monroe alive.

could be the vital clue that needs to be solved if anyone is to unravel the truth behind Marilyn's death.

SKEPTICALLY SPEAKING

It is easy to connect a lot of disparate dots in a revealing manner when it comes to the death of Marilyn Monroe.

Intimate relationships with the highest officials in the land, FBI files, and links to the Mafia are all suggestive but do not necessarily mean that there was a conspiracy. By August 1962, Marilyn was a psychologically damaged alcoholic: neither an accidental drug overdose nor a deliberate act of suicide would necessarily have been out of character for Marilyn at that stage of her life. The screen goddess always had a legendary quality about her during life, and the conspiracy theories may just be an extension of the inevitable Hollywood myth-making process that doesn't stop just because the star concerned does.

7 Jim Morrison—Death or Disappearance

Lizard King, Rock God, shamanic spirit of the sixties. Without a doubt one of the biggest personalities of the music scene of his time, Jim Morrison always had a mythical quality about him. This appears to have done nothing but grow since his death in a Paris apartment on July 4, 1971. In fact, many conspiracy theorists feel his death is the greatest myth of Morrison's life; some believe it would take more than heart failure to rob the world of such a larger-than-life character.

After nearly five years of fame, Jim took a break from the Doors after they had fulfilled their contractual obligation to Elektra Records by delivering the seminal album *L.A. Woman*. They may have been a little disgruntled that he left during the mixing stages of the LP, but this was not the end of the group and they fully expected him to return from Paris.

Morrison was bored with life in L.A. and sought out Paris as it was a place to inspire him—a romantic city of art and poetry. He mentioned to some people his desire to purchase an old church in the south of France so he could renovate it and use it as a permanent base from which he would only venture back to the hustle of America when business demanded. He took with him his scrapbooks filled with poetry and ideas, reels from three of the films he was working on, and plans to write a play.

He and his long-term girlfriend, Pamela Courson, quickly established a home for themselves in a Paris apartment. Jim wrote, appeared as an extra in a play, drank vast quantities of alcohol, and began to enjoy the freedom of not being recognized every time he stepped outside his door. He often expressed opinions during this time that he felt like he needed to change the direction of his life—it was clear that he wanted to get away from things and that he wanted to travel.

While years of drinking, drug-taking, and other forms of physical self-abuse had made their mark on Morrison, his unexpected death—recorded as resulting from heart failure—took many by surprise. It also inspired doubts in others that he was actually dead, doubts that intensified when one or two curious facts ended up in the public domain.

THE STRANGE PART

No one who knew Morrison really well, other than his girl-friend, actually saw him dead. Even after the official death certificate had been produced, some of his friends and family members doubted that Morrison really had shuffled off this mortal coil.

THE USUAL SUSPECTS

Jim Morrison

It is rumored that some people who had contractual arrangements with him in the music business immediately assumed that his death was staged in order to facilitate an easy release from troublesome and binding contracts that he would have had to fulfill had he lived. Established facts also show that Morrison was enjoying the anonymity of his life in Paris and he took great care to ensure that there were no new publicity pictures showing what he looked like after he left Los Angeles. so he would not be disturbed. He talked of escaping his fame. Faking his death may have been the perfect way to achieve this aim.

Friends of Jim Morrison

Some suspect that the confusion over Morrison's death stems from the notion that certain people wanted to disguise that he died of a drug overdose. Chief conspirator in this intrigue would have been his partner, the late Pamela Courson, who was purported to have had his body removed from the infamous Parisian junkie joint the Rock 'n' Roll Circus to their apartment in order to avoid a scandal and police questioning. This might explain her actions after she "found" Morrison unconscious in the bath—her first few telephone calls were to friends, not to the paramedics.

THE UNUSUAL SUSPECTS

The FBI

The FBI had kept Morrison under surveillance when he had been in the United States. Files and memoranda to the then director of the FBI—the infamous J. Edgar Hoover—make mention of him trying to "provoke chaos." The bureau certainly kept tabs on those they thought capable of inciting rebellion or drug use among the young, and on people who were in contact with those thought to be subversive—two counts on which Morrison definitely qualified for attention. It should not come as too much of a surprise that some conspiracy theorists have conjectured that the FBI was involved in the strange circumstances surrounding Morrison's (alleged) death because they wished to ensure that Morrison did not return to the USA and start provoking that chaos again.

Worldwide Witch Cult

Morrison had an intense interest in witchcraft and is said to have been an active participant in at least one witch cult. It is claimed by some conspiracy theorists that Morrison was abducted as part of a dark plot to obtain the living representation of Dionysus—the Greek god of fertility and wine—for ritual sacrifice.

MOST CONVINCING EVIDENCE

Though it is easy to be jaded when hearing conspiracies such as these, there is some convincing evidence to suggest that all is not as it seems with the Morrison case. No autopsy ever was performed. People who knew him well—including band member Ray Manzarek—believed that he was still alive and Morrison's own remarks that he wanted to escape the life of a rock star are all telling. However, the most convincing evidence is that more than a week after he had been "buried," Pamela Courson told a journalist working for United Press International that Morrison was staying at a special clinic outside Paris to convalesce from illness.

MOST MYSTERIOUS FACT

It is effectively impossible to exhume Morrison's body to prove he is actually dead. Apart from needing the family's approval, you also need the consent from seven French cardinals, who can each demand a right of veto and who are renowned for disagreeing on this type of matter. This is the case with all exhumations from the Père Lachaise Cemetery, and Jim had speculated he might be buried there.

SKEPTICALLY SPEAKING

Toward the end of his life, Jim Morrison was an overweight, chain-smoking alcoholic who lived very dangerously by keeping up his intake of narcotics while also taking prescription medicine to combat his asthma. The death of someone in those circumstances is hardly surprising—it is pretty much inevitable.

8 IS THE KING STILL ALIVE?

The official version: Elvis died on August 16, 1977, from an overdose of drugs. He died sitting on the toilet, with his pants around his ankles, a bloated and burnt-out version of his former self, and his body is now in residence at Graceland.

The conspiracy version has it that the death of the "King of Rock 'n' Roll" was an elaborate hoax on the public and that the original Hound Dog is still alive and being spotted by numerous people across the globe.

It has to be agreed that his death did come as a shock—forty-two is an early age to die, and Elvis did have a history of pulling off some rather bizarre and eccentric stunts. There are certainly some mysterious elements surrounding his alleged death.

THE STRANGE PART

A mere two hours after his death was announced, a man looking remarkably like Elvis bought a ticket for Buenos Aires using the name John Burrows. This was a pseudonym that the King himself had used quite a few times, notably on the occasion he flew to Washington to meet President Nixon. It was on the same visit to D.C. that he went to the headquarters of the FBI, announced his desire to inform on fellow show business performers and became an honorary member of the Bureau of Narcotics and Dangerous Drugs. It is alleged that John Burrows flew out of the USA on special State Department papers and this has fueled speculation that Burrows was none other than Presley making his escape to a new life.

THE USUAL SUSPECTS

Elvis Presley

The hottest contender for the instigator of the conspiracy is none other than Elvis himself. The King definitely felt like a prisoner of his own fame and was tired of riding in the trunks of cars to avoid detection and of not being able to get proper medical attention because any hospital he was in would be overwhelmed by fans. At forty-two, he was going downhill and was too proud to go out with a whimper. Elvis had already once faked his death by setting up a deceptive

shooting, so it is not impossible that he staged a more final fake death.

The FBI

Elvis had lost a vast amount of money in bad deals with companies that had close links to the Mafia. There is a lot of speculation that the King decided to collaborate with the federal government to help expose gangsters. To ensure his protection, the FBI had to fake his death and provide him with a new life as part of a very unusual witness relocation program.

THE UNUSUAL SUSPECTS

Burger Chain Companies

Could the faked death of Elvis be part of an innovative and radical marketing scam? It has been suggested that the frequent sighting of Elvis cooking fries in numerous backwoods burger joints—which then become very popular, acting as shrines and magnets for Elvis fans—is a joint plan between the King and the burger chain companies. Elvis gets to live a life free from the pressures of fame and is paid in cheeseburgers, while the fast-food bosses get to increase business in their quieter establishments.

Two conspiracy favorites, President Nixon and Elvis, exchange a special handshake.

New World Order

Since Elvis allegedly bought the farm, it has become clear to many cultural observers that he is well on the way to becoming a religious figure. Books comparing him to Christ have hit the U.S. best-seller lists, sightings of Elvis can be seen as similar to spiritual visions, and there is no denying that many fans have shrines to the King and describe visiting Graceland in terms of making a pilgrimage. If you are of a paranoid bent, you may want to consider the claims that the Elvis conspiracy was instigated by the New World Order (NWO) as their attempt to lay the groundwork for a future new religion. Has Elvis been cryogenically frozen by the NWO to be revived as the globe's new messiah when it comes to power?

MJ-12

Every Elvis conspiracy is more than a little odd, but the suggested link between the King and Roswell—where in 1947 a UFO was supposed to have crashed and the military recovered alien bodies—is bizarre even by Elvis standards. It has been claimed that the military photographer who captured Elvis on film for U.S. Marine publicity purposes was a man called Barret who just happened to be the U.S. Army photographer brought in to record the dead alien's autopsies. Conspiracy buffs, with a love for the territory of deep weird, have it that the photographer sent Elvis a copy of those alien pictures with the fatal consequence that MJ-12—the guys behind the UFO cover-up—had to silence the King.

MOST CONVINCING EVIDENCE

Aside from the frequently quoted fact that "Elvis" is an anagram of "lives," possibly the most convincing evidence surrounds the 900-pound coffin with a built-in air-chilling unit in which Elvis was buried. How did the Presley family manage to obtain a 900-pound, custom-made coffin ready for a funeral held on the day after his death and still fail to follow the more basic request from Elvis, such as being buried next to his mother? In the days leading up to his alleged death, the King is said to have made odd nocturnal visits to several funeral homes. Why?

MOST MYSTERIOUS FACT

The King's name is spelled wrongly on his headstone. His full name was Elvis Aron Presley, but on his grave his middle name is spelled incorrectly with an additional 'a.' The unique spelling of Aron was an important Presley family tradition. When he was born, Aron was misspelled as Aaron on his birth certificate and Elvis's father went to great lengths to correct the recording of his son's name. It seems very odd that Elvis's family would have allowed this error to occur on the King's tombstone.

SKEPTICALLY SPEAKING

The King is dead—get over it.

9 DEATH OF PRINCESS DI

The death of Princess Diana was an event that affected people across the planet. Britain grieved; the world grieved. Even people who had never devoted any real attention to the British royal family felt deep emotion at the tragic circumstances that robbed the world of someone who qualified as a global cultural icon.

At first it appeared to be nothing more than a simple tragic accident. Diana had enjoyed a romantic meal with her lover, Dodi Al Fayed, at the Ritz Hotel, owned by his father, Mohamed Al Fayed. A little before midnight the couple left, accompanied by Diana's bodyguard—Trevor Rees-Jones. To escape thirty paparazzi parked outside, they went out via the back door. The chauffeur of their bulletproof Mercedes-Benz was Henri Paul, the Ritz Hotel's head of security.

The car sped away, and a tourist captured the scene on video as an innocent-looking Citroen followed and the

Grief swept the land in the wake of Princess Diana's death.

paparazzi, realizing they had been duped, began to give chase on their motorcycles. After a few minutes' pursuit, the Mercedes entered the Pont de l'Alma tunnel at high speed, and all we know is that Diana, Dodi, and Henri failed to emerge from it with their lives. It took the French investigation several years to produce an official version of events. Not surprisingly, they supported the instant verdict from the world's media that it was a woeful auto accident caused by the combination of a drunk driver, pursuing paparazzi, and a failure to wear seat belts.

The first public suggestion that there was a conspiracy to kill Princess Diana surfaced on the BBC World Service a couple of days after the unfortunate events of August 31, 1997. In bizarre propagandist tones, the BBC made pains to deride a speech made by Libyan leader Colonel Muammar Qaddafi in which he claimed that the "accident" was a joint French and British conspiracy because they did not want Diana to marry a Muslim man. Conspiracy theories began circulating on the night of her death, most of them speculating on how strange it was that on the day she died, Diana had already told one major British national newspaper to prepare for an amazing announcement.

THE STRANGE PART

The queen intervened to clear Diana's former butler, Paul Burrell, when he was on trial at the Old Bailey just before he was about to take the stand and possibly reveal a number of uncomfortable facts about the princess in November 2002. It later emerged that after Diana's death, the queen had spoken at length to Burrell. Sounding like the most paranoid of conspiracy theorists and using dialogue that would not have been out of place in *The X-Files*, she warned Burrell to be careful, saying, "There are powers at work in this country which we have no knowledge about." The warning led Burrell to wait until October 2003 to make public the fact that Diana had written him a note ten months before she died. It stated: "This particular phase of my life is the most dangerous. 'X' is planning an accident in my car, brake failure and serious head injuries in order to make the path clear for Charles to marry." The princess's startling prescience has heightened the belief that she was a victim of a conspiracy, not a tragic accident.

THE USUAL SUSPECTS

MI6

Sworn to protect the British crown, a renegade faction within MI6 is alleged to have taken it upon itself to rid the royal family of the one woman who looked capable of destroying the monarchy by exposing the hypocrisy of the Windsors. That she may have been pregnant, about to convert to Islam, and marry the son of establishment bogeyman Mohammed Al Fayed may have been the final factors that made them decide she must die.

Military-Industrial Complex

Diana had waged a one-woman war against the evils of land mines, in doing so risking her personal safety and earning strident political criticism in the United Kingdom as a "loose cannon." While the military-industrial complex makes more money from disposing of land mines than it does selling them, it may have feared the possibility of Diana turning her attention to the arms industry in general.

Clearly, it would have been in the military-industrial complex's best interest to wipe out someone who could have turned into the world's most powerful peace campaigner.

Also suspected: the CIA; Mossad; Islamic Fundamentalists; Saddam Hussein; the Freemasons (she died under a bridge— an important Masonic symbol); and the IRA.

THE UNUSUAL SUSPECTS

The Committee

The Committee is a rumored Anglo-American cabal made up of intelligence agency operatives from the United States and Great Britain. Supposedly headquartered in Bristol, England, the Committee is apparently a tool of an even more clandestine group that wants the special relationship between the United States and Britain to develop into a union of both powers. Possibly Diana's massive popularity, willingness to tackle the establishment on sensitive issues, and possible pregnancy persuaded the group she could be a dangerous opponent to its cryptic schemes.

Princess Diana

Another bizarre hypothesis is that Diana staged her own death so she and Dodi could live free from the glare of publicity. Not surprisingly, there's little hard evidence to support this piece of wishful thinking.

MOST CONVINCING EVIDENCE

Claims have been made that Henri Paul's blood-alcohol level was three times over the legal limit. A second blood test ordered by his disbelieving family showed a level of carbon monoxide in his body that was not only lethal, but also would have entered his bloodstream before he got into the car. The security video from the Ritz that night does not show him as a drunk or reeling from carbon monoxide poisoning. The mystery of Henri Paul deepens further with the revelation that he deposited more than 164,000 francs into his bank account shortly before he died. When, in 2003, it was announced that British inquests were to be held into the deaths of Diana and Dodi, conspiracy theorists were dismayed to find out they would be held by Surrey coroner Michael Burgess. As he is also coroner for the royal household, many doubt that the truth will emerge at the inquests.

MOST MYSTERIOUS FACT

The crash happened in the Pont de l'Alma tunnel, which was built over a site used in the time of the Merovingian dynasty (between 500 and 751 CE) as a sacred ritual area. Some secret societies, such as the Prieure de Sion and the Templars, claim that the Merovingian and all true European royalty—including Diana Spencer's family—are connected to the pagan cult of Diana. It is odd that Britain's Queen of Hearts may have died on a former site of worship for the goddess whose name she was given.

SKEPTICALLY SPEAKING

Even if Diana was pregnant, that does not mean there was a conspiracy to kill her. Driving at high speed through Paris is dangerous enough without being pursued by a pack of motorcycle paparazzi. Add a barrage of camera flashes to a chase conducted at more than 120 miles per hour (193 kilometers per hour) when the passengers are not wearing seat belts and you no longer need a conspiracy to explain a fatal crash. Faced with a tragedy such as Diana's death, it is not surprising that some people cannot accept it as a mere random accident. The car crash in Paris may be the perfect example of why some conspiracy theories come into being: if they did not exist we'd have to face the banality and indiscriminate nature of death.

10 SID VICIOUS

When New York's finest entered Room 100 of the Chelsea Hotel on October 12, 1978, they discovered a horrific sight. Lying beneath the bathroom sink, clad only in her underwear and covered in blood, was Nancy Spungen. She was dead, killed by a single knife blow to her abdomen. Her boyfriend, himself in a drug-induced muddle, was Sid Vicious, bass player with the then notorious punk band the Sex Pistols. He was charged with Spungen's murder and later released on $50,000 bail.

The romance between Vicious (born John Simon Ritchie) and Nancy Spungen was the stuff rock 'n' roll nightmares are made of. After being recruited by his best friend John Lydon—aka Johnny Rotten—to replace the existing bass player in his band, the Sex Pistols (named after Malcolm McLaren and Vivienne Westwood's London boutique, Sex), Vicious soon found himself at the epicenter of a pop-culture phenomenon.

The band was already notorious in England. Spearheading the UK punk movement, the Pistols originally had been put together by McLaren to specifically appeal to the disaffected youth of England. With songs calculated to infuriate all the wrong people (anyone over thirty), the Pistols tore through England on the breaking wave of punk rock. With songs such as "Anarchy in the UK" and "God Save the Queen," coupled with outrageous outbursts on television and other media, they were nothing short of a slow-motion atom bomb about to shake the foundations of pop culture worldwide.

Which wasn't bad for Vicious, considering there was debate about whether he ever knew how to play the bass at all. Instead, he relied more on image: cutting himself with razor blades, spitting blood, and even urinating while on stage. The anarchy poster boy, beloved by many newborn punk rockers, he proved irresistible to one fan, an American girl named Nancy Spungen, who came over to England with the express purpose of capturing the heart—or anything else—of a Pistol. She and Vicious met in 1977 and soon became lovers, careening into an affair riddled with drug abuse. Vicious's love of Spungen, coupled with Spungen's abrasive personality, became so intense that it began to tear the band apart. When the Pistols' ill-fated American tour ended abruptly, with lead singer Johnny Rotten returning to England in disgust, Vicious stayed with Spungen, finally ending up in New York's Chelsea Hotel. After Spungen's death, out of

Love's young dream? Sid and Nancy were punk rock's highest profile couple.

despair, Vicious tried to commit suicide and carved his entire forearm with a knife. Somehow surviving that, he finally succumbed to a heroin overdose (with heroin brought for him by his mother, fearing that her son might get caught in a police sting) on February 2, 1979. He was only twenty-one.

THE STRANGE PART

Theories have arisen over the possibility of a conspiracy concerning Vicious's death. There are dark hints that there was more at hand than the tragic deaths of two heroin addicts, and even murmurs that Vicious may not have killed Spungen at all.

THE USUAL SUSPECTS

Unknown Residents of the Chelsea Hotel

Keeping in mind the drug-hazed state of Vicious and of Spungen before her death, it's entirely probable that some-one other than Vicious may have killed Spungen. In his befuddled state of mind, he may not even have been aware of the murder. The perpetrators, worried about the truth coming out if Vicious's case went to trial, ensured his silence by making sure that his mother brought a lethally cut dose of heroin for her son.

Former Associates

Some conspiracy theorists feel that former friends and associates of Vicious's may have had him supplied with a hit of lethal "hot" heroin. This was meant as an unusual act of mercy to spare him having to face the living hell of a long prison sentence served out in New York's most notorious jail, a place he would not have been vicious enough to survive.

THE UNUSUAL SUSPECTS
The CIA and FBI

Just as the murder of John Lennon may be attributed to a mutual desire by the CIA and FBI to remove any pop-culture figure that could possibly lead the population to revolt, Vicious might have been killed because he represented punk anarchy in all its glory. He had the potential to give American youth a role model that made the young Elvis look the model of respectability. Indeed, some theories suggest that Vicious could have been a simple trial run of a CIA or FBI rubout program before attention moved on to the more difficult task of removing Lennon. Both men died, coincidentally, in New York.

MOST CONVINCING EVIDENCE

However tormented and tortuous the relationship between Spungen and Vicious, it was painfully clear to all those around him that he needed her, perhaps more than anything or anyone else. Regardless of his state of intoxication, to kill her would seem completely out of character. In telephone conversations with Spungen's mother after Nancy's death, Vicious never made any comments about it at all. If he were as guilt-ridden over killing her as we would be led to believe, would he be able to hide his pain that well? In all other things, Vicious was not known as a paragon of restraint.

MOST MYSTERIOUS FACT

While Vicious's mother was returning her son's ashes to England, John Lydon claims that she dropped the urn in Heathrow, scattering them across the airport floor. A significant proportion of them were sucked into the ventilation system.

SKEPTICALLY SPEAKING

Although it would be romantic to think that all the rock stars who die young do so because the "powers that be" want them dead, there are times when death is simply a tragic end to a tragic story. Sid Vicious was a young man with next to no musical talent, who was simply in the right place at the right time looking the right way. When McLaren created the Sex Pistols, he wanted stars he could manipulate and he got that with Vicious. Unlike general perceptions of John Lennon and Jim Morrison, the idea that Vicious could ever be a threat to American society is ludicrous. He was the "It Boy" of the punk generation, and nothing more. If his death was to be chalked down to anything, it should be heroin, and the equally dangerous drug of media exposure.

GLOSSARY

Antichrist The description of the antagonist who was expected by the early Church to set himself up against Christ in the last days before the Second Coming.

audacious Fearlessly daring or recklessly bold.

bogeyman A terrifying or dreaded person.

cabal A group of people secretly plotting something or united to bring about some form of intrigue.

conspiriologists Conspiracy theorists who have taken an interest in researching the truth behind various dark plots.

enigmatic Of or resembling a puzzle; something that is ambiguous or inexplicable.

extradition The legal surrender of an alleged criminal to the jurisdiction of another state, country, or government for trial.

Freedom of Information Act (FOIA) An act requiring U.S. agencies to provide citizens access to public records on request (some exceptions are permitted, including materials for national defense, confidential personnel and financial data, and law enforcement files). If people are denied access to requested information, they may sue for disclosure and a court can determine whether information has been improperly classified.

Generation X People born between 1965 and 1975;
      generally used to describe the generation consisting of
      people born after baby boomers.

grunge A kind of rock music that incorporates elements of
      punk rock and heavy metal.

maharishi A Hindu teacher of mystical knowledge.

military-industrial complex (MIC) An informal alliance of the
      military and related government departments with defense
      industries that is held to influence government policy.

MK-Ultra The acronym for Manufacturing Killers Utilizing
      Lethal Tradecraft Requiring Assassinations; the code
      name for a CIA mind control research project lasting
      from the 1950s through the 1970s.

paragon A model or pattern of excellence or perfection; a
      peerless example.

synchronicity The quality of being, happening, or arising at
      precisely the same time.

For More Information

Central Intelligence Agency (CIA)
Office of Public Affairs
Washington, DC 20505
(703) 482-0623
Web site: http://www.cia.gov

Federal Bureau of Investigation (FBI)
J. Edgar Hoover Building
935 Pennsylvania Avenue NW
Washington, DC 20535-0001
(202) 324-3000
Web site: http://www.fbi.gov

John F. Kennedy Presidential Library and Museum
Columbia Point
Boston, MA 02125
(866) JFK-1960
Web site: http://www.jfklibrary.org

National Archives and Records Administration
8601 Adelphi Road
College Park, MD 20740-6001
(866) 272-6272
Web site: http://www.archives.gov

WEB SITES

Due to the changing nature of Internet links, Rosen Publishing has developed an online list of Web sites related to the subject of this book. This site is updated regularly. Please use this link to access the list:

http://www.rosenlinks.com/mc/uncm

FOR FURTHER READING

Belzer, Richard. *UFOs, JFK, and Elvis: Conspiracies You Don't Have to Be Crazy to Believe.* New York, NY: Ballantine, 2000.

Bondesan, Jan. *The Great Pretenders: The True Stories Behind Famous Historical Mysteries.* New York, NY: W. W. Norton, 2004.

Burnett, Thom, ed. *Conspiracy Encyclopedia: The Encyclopedia of Conspiracy Theories.* New York, NY: Chamberlain Bros., 2005.

Hidell, Al, and Joan D'Arc. *The Complete Conspiracy Reader: From the Deaths of JFK and John Lennon to Government-Sponsored Alien Cover-Ups.* New York, NY: MJF Books, 2003.

Knight, Peter. *Conspiracy Culture: From Kennedy to the X-Files.* Oxford, England: Routledge, 2001.

Kurtz, Michael L. *The JFK Assassination Debates: Lone Gunman Versus Conspiracy.* Lawrence, KS: University Press of Kansas, 2006.

Levy, Joel. *The Little Book of Conspiracies: 50 Reasons to Be Paranoid.* New York, NY: Thunder's Mouth Press, 2005.

Livingstone, Harrison Edward, and Robert J. Groden. *High Treason: The Assassination of JFK and the Case for Conspiracy.* New York, NY: Carroll & Graf, 1998.

Smith, Matthew. *Marilyn's Last Words: Her Secret Tapes and Mysterious Death.* New York, NY: Carroll & Graf, 2004.

Tuckett, Kate. *Conspiracy Theories.* New York, NY: Berkley, 2005.

Wallace, Max, and Ian Halperin. *Love & Death: The Murder of Kurt Cobain.* New York, NY: Atria, 2004.

Index

PHOTO CREDITS

Cover *(left)*, pp. 15, 29, 43, 56 Bettmann/Corbis; cover *(right)*, p. 61 Liba Taylor/Corbis; p. 7 S.I.N./Corbis; p. 9 Denis Griskin/Corbis; pp. 22, 25 Collection Cinéma/Photos12.com; p. 36 Huton-Deutsch Collection/Corbis; p. 46 Library of Congress; p. 68 Sunset Boulevard/Corbis.

Designer: Tom Forget

DATE DUE

Demco, Inc. 38-293